WHAT WOULD YOU DO?

Written by Michele Spirn and Rebecca Stark
Illustrated by Karen Birchak

ISBN 0-910857-44-X

© Educational Impressions, Inc. 1987
Revised edition © 2006

EDUCATIONAL IMPRESSIONS, INC.
Hawthorne, New Jersey 07507

Printed in the U.S.A.

Table of Contents

To the Teacher

The purpose of this workbook is to motivate children to look at alternatives before reaching decisions as to what's right and what's wrong—at least for them. The open-ended stories prompt children to think about their own feelings and experiences as they identify with the characters in the stories. Youngsters are encouraged to develop a standard set of values by which to live.

The activities which follow each story were especially designed to help develop students' critical- and creative-thinking skills.

I Wish I Hadn't Said That

This had been Neil's first year at his new school. He had made a lot of good friends and was very happy. The school term would end next week. Neil and his friends were looking forward to spending their summer vacation together.

"You should see how great the town pool is," Jenny said to Neil.

"Yeah," Trevor added, "I can't wait to practice my dives!"

"Remember my great dive from the high board?" Peter asked proudly. "I must admit I was kind of scared the first time I tried it."

Then Peter's younger sister, Chris, took out a card. It was the beginner's Red Cross card she earned last year. She told everyone that she had to pass a swim test to get it.

Trevor told everyone that he was working on his intermediate card. He only had one or two more requirements to pass when the pool closed last year. Trevor was certain he would earn the card as soon as the pool opened.

Neil just listened. He was very quiet. In fact, he was embarrassed. He had never learned how to swim! Now he realized that his friends were good swimmers, and he couldn't swim a stroke. He felt terrible.

"Do you have your intermediate card yet, Neil?" Jenny asked innocently.

Neil was too embarrassed to admit that he couldn't swim. "I'll be getting it soon," he mumbled.

Neil's friends continued to discuss their plans for the summer. The more they spoke, the more uncomfortable Neil became. Now he had two reasons to feel terrible. Not only was he the only one who couldn't swim, but he had lied to his friends! Finally, he said that he had to go home.

When Neil got home, his mother greeted him. "I've been waiting for you to come home," she said excitedly. "There's a letter for you! It's from your scout leader!"

Neil read the letter anxiously. It said that his troop would be going on a camping trip to Hickory Lake. The letter described the cookouts, sports, hikes, woodcraft, and other activities there would be. It really sounded great!

That is, it sounded great until he read the last paragraph! Then it hit him. There would be swim tests that every camper would have to take. After the tests, the campers would be put into groups according to their ability. Then they would be given swimming lessons.

In a way, Neil was happy about the lessons. He had wanted to learn how to swim for a long time. Now he would have the chance; however, he was afraid of what his friends would say when they found out he had lied. Trevor and Peter were in his troop. They would be right there when he took the test.

If only he hadn't lied. He was sorry that he told them he was working on his intermediate card. He wished he had been honest with them.

Neil's mother wondered why he didn't seem happy about the camping trip. She reminded him of all the times he had begged for swimming lessons. Now he would be able to have them.

"I am happy," he cried and ran to his room.

Of course, his mother was right. Neil was not happy. In fact, he was miserable. He thought of pretending to be sick the day they were to leave, but he really didn't want to miss the whole trip. The cook-outs, hikes, and other activities sounded like so much fun! Besides, Neil knew that sooner or later his friends would learn the truth. His family would be going to the town pool and he'd have to go too.

Neil thought about telling them he lied. He practiced what he would say while looking in the mirror.

Neil was afraid that the other kids would laugh at him for not knowing how to swim. Worse yet, when they found out that he had lied, they might not want to be his friends. "Maybe I'll just go on the trip and hope for the best," he said to his image in the mirror. Neil was confused and worried. He didn't know what to do.

What would you do if you were Neil?

Write three possible endings to this story.

Ending #1

_____

_____

_____

_____

_____

Ending #2

_____

_____

_____

_____

_____

Ending #3

_____

_____

_____

_____

_____

Put a ✔ next to the ending that describes what you would do if you were Neil.

Suppose Neil had told the truth from the start. Complete this conversation as you think it would have occurred.

Jenny: Do you have your intermediate card yet, Neil?

Neil: I don't know how to swim.

Jenny: _____

_____

_____

Make a list of the reasons people lie.

_____

_____

_____

_____

Do you think there are ever good reasons to lie? Draw a picture of a situation in which the "liar" has good intentions.

Do you think the person in your picture should have lied? Tell why or why not.

_____

_____

_____

Unscramble the "Lies"

Unscramble the letters to form words about different forms of lying.

1. ile   = _____

2. ibf   = _____

3. lftuthahr   = _____

4. dooheslaf   = _____

5. ncepdetio   = _____

6. utuntrh   = _____

7. itewhile   = _____ _____

These are extra tough! Three cheers for anyone who gets these!

8. varateciepr = _____

9. quieovtcae = _____

10. juperry   = _____

The Whole Truth And Nothing But The Truth

Analyze each of the following situations. Decide in each if not telling the truth is just as bad as lying.

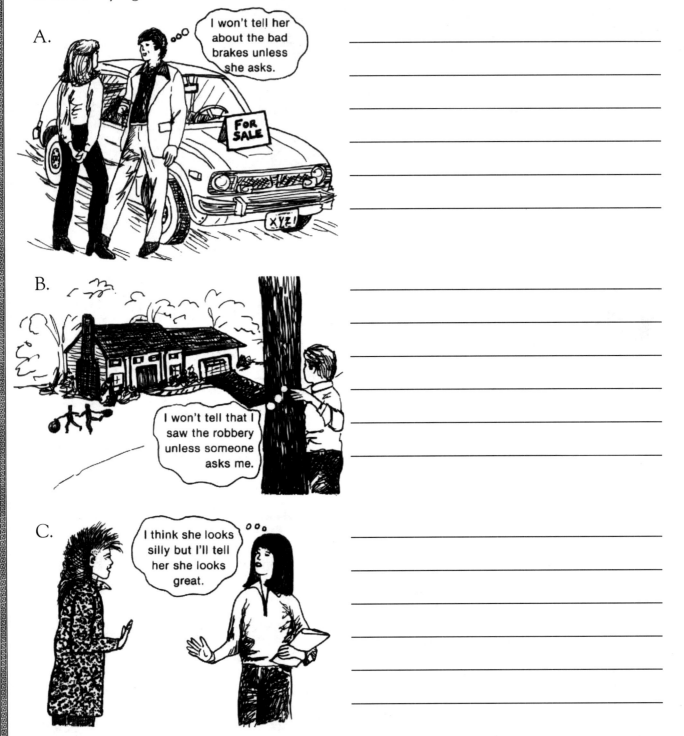

A.

B.

C.

Finders, Keepers?

When Jennifer left school one afternoon, her friends were waiting for her in the playground. "We're going to the new ice cream parlor on Main Street," Melissa told her. "Do you want to come with us?"

Jennifer was tempted to say yes, but she turned down their offer. "I'm saving my money to buy a camera," she explained. "It's on sale. I'm going there now to take another look at it."

Jennifer wanted this camera more than anything else. It was a digital camera. You can see what the picture will look like as soon as you shoot it. She thought that $109.95 was a good price for such a terrific camera. She had already saved over $85.00.

Of course, she hadn't been able to spend money on things like movies, candy and ice cream like the other kids. Sometimes she wondered if it was worth the trouble. When she thought about all the great pictures she would take, she decided it was.

Jennifer walked to the store. It was near the school. She looked at the camera one more time. Soon it would be hers.

On her way home Jennifer walked through the playground. She wanted to ride on the swings. As she swung high in the air, she noticed something on the ground below. She got off the swing to see what it was.

It was a wallet. Jennifer looked inside to see if there was anything to show whose it was. There was no identification, but there was something else—a twenty-dollar bill. She looked around, but no one was there.

Jennifer decided to take the wallet to the Lost and Found Department at school. When she tried the doors, however, they were all locked. It was getting late. Jennifer put the wallet in her back pack and headed for home. She would bring it in tomorrow.

By the time Jennifer arrived home, she had forgotten all about finding the wallet. She went straight to her room to count the money she had saved. Actually, she knew exactly how much she had—eighty-five dollars and fifty cents. She still needed twenty-nine dollars and forty-five cents. Jennifer wished that she didn't have such a long way to go. As much as she wanted the camera, she was tired of not being able to go anywhere or buy anything.

Just then she remembered the twenty-dollar bill she had found. If she kept it, she would have almost enough money to buy the camera. Jennifer took the wallet from her back pack and removed the twenty-dollar bill.

Jennifer tried to convince herself that what she was doing really wasn't stealing. After all, she found the wallet; she didn't steal it. Everyone knows the old saying, "finders, keepers–losers, weepers." Besides, it wasn't her fault that the doors to the Lost and Found Department were locked!

Jennifer had mixed feelings. On the one hand, she knew no one had seen her pick up the wallet. It would be so easy just to use the money. On the other hand, she knew how badly she would feel if she had lost her wallet.

Jennifer didn't know what to do.

What would you do if you were Jennifer?

Write three possible endings to this story.

Ending #1

_____

_____

_____

_____

_____

Ending #2

_____

_____

_____

_____

_____

Ending #3

_____

_____

_____

_____

_____

Put a ✔ next to the ending that describes what you would do if you were Jennifer.

Do you think Jennifer did all she could to find the owner? What else could she do?

_____

_____

_____

_____

How do you think Jennifer will feel if she uses the money she found?

_____

_____

_____

_____

How do you think she will feel if she returns the money and saves all of the money herself?

_____

_____

_____

_____

Make a list of adjectives that would describe how you would feel if you lost something that was important to you. Then make a list of adjectives that would describe how you would feel if it were returned.

_____   _____

_____   _____

_____   _____

_____   _____

_____   _____

_____ *For Sale*

List as many ways as you can think of that someone your age could earn extra money.

Summer:

_____   _____

_____   _____

_____   _____

Fall:

_____   _____

_____   _____

_____   _____

Spring:

_____   _____

_____   _____

_____   _____

Winter:

_____   _____

_____   _____

_____   _____

All Seasons:

_____   _____

_____   _____

_____   _____

Decide how you would earn extra money if you wanted to save for something special. Create a poster advertising your product or service. Use the space below to sketch your ad.

Is It Stealing If...

Decide whether you would be stealing in each situation.

Situation #1: You're at a baseball game. The boy in the row ahead is leaving. You see that he has left his mitt under the seat. You say nothing. As soon as he's gone, you put the mitt in your bag. About a half hour later, the boy returns. He asks if anyone's seen his mitt. You say nothing.
Are you stealing?

_____

_____

_____

_____

Situation #2: You are flying alone on an airplane for the first time. Your parents want to know if you've arrived safely, but they don't really have to talk to you. They tell you to call person-to-person and ask for yourself. That way they'll know you're safe but they will say you're not there, and there will be no charge for the call.
Are you stealing?

_____

_____

_____

_____

Situation #3: You're in the supermarket. The clerk has given you too much change. You notice but you don't say anything. You figure that if he realizes his mistake, you can always pretend you didn't notice.
Are you stealing?

_____

_____

_____

_____

To Tell or Not to Tell

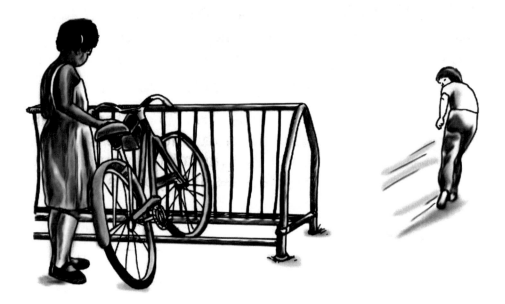

It was late by the time Denise got out of school. She had stayed after class to help the teacher. She was glad that she had ridden her bike to school. At least it wouldn't take her too long to get home.

All of a sudden she noticed that someone was fooling around with her bicycle. At first she couldn't see who it was. Then Denise realized that it was Joe, one of her classmates. When he saw her coming, he ran away.

Joe was always playing practical jokes. Denise wondered what crazy stunt he was up to now. She remembered that just this afternoon during recess Joe offered her a candy bar. When she opened it, it was only an empty wrapper. Right after that he tried to scare her with a rubber snake.

Denise decided that she'd better look in her basket. He might have put something in it. To her surprise, she found nothing unusual.

Denise thought that she must have been wrong about Joe. She hopped on her bike and headed for home. Before she got very far, however, she realized that something was wrong. Denise got off her bike. Her brakes were too loose to ride. She'd never be able to stop on the steep hills.

Denise was puzzled. She knew that the brakes were okay on the way to school. Then she realized that Joe must have done something to them. That's why he ran away when he saw her.

Denise couldn't ride the bike. It was too dangerous. She started to walk home, pushing the bike along side her. As she walked, she grew more and more angry. Joe was supposed to be her friend. Why would he do such a thing? Did he think this was just another practical joke?

She pushed the bike up the hill. As she pushed, she thought about how lucky she was that she had noticed that something was wrong. "I really could have gotten hurt!" Denise said out loud.

Denise planned to tell her parents what Joe did as soon as she got home. They'd be sure to call his parents. Maybe she would tell her teacher, too. After all, he was on school grounds when he did it. She thought he deserved to be punished. Then she remembered something her parents had told her. They said it wasn't nice to tattle on her friends.

Once Denise told her mother that her younger sister was reading instead of sleeping. She thought she was being helpful. Instead of thanking her, her mother told her not to be a tattletale! Denise also remembered when her sister had told her mother that Denise had eaten some cookies her mother had made for the bake sale. She thought her sister was a tattletale for getting her into trouble. Maybe she shouldn't tell anyone who did this to her bicycle. Everyone in her class might call her a tattletale if she told.

On the other hand, this was more serious than eating a few cookies. She could have gotten hurt! Besides, her bicycle was expensive. Who was going to pay to have it fixed?

Denise was sure that her parents would ask her what happened to the bike. She didn't want to lie.

Denise didn't know what to do.

What would you do if you were Denise?

Write three possible endings to this story.

Ending #1

_____

_____

_____

_____

_____

Ending #2

_____

_____

_____

_____

_____

Ending #3

_____

_____

_____

_____

_____

Put a ✔ next to the ending that describes what you would do if you were Denise.

Analyze the difference between what Joe did and a "practical joke."

_____

_____

_____

Analyze the difference between tattling and responsible telling.

_____

_____

_____

If it were up to you, would you punish Joe? Why or why not? If you would punish him, what would his punishment be?

_____

_____

_____

From what you know about Joe, do you think he wanted Denise to get hurt?

_____

_____

_____

Did anyone ever tell on you when you did something wrong? Describe how you felt. At the time did you think that person was a tattletale? Do you still think so?

_____

_____

_____

If you were Denise, would you forgive Joe? If yes, under what circumstances would you forgive him?

_____

_____

_____

I Would Tell If...

In which of these situations would you "tell on" the person involved. Circle yes or no for each..

1. You see someone stealing your friend's bicycle.   Yes—No

2. You see someone stealing a stranger's bicycle.   Yes—No

3. Your classmate hasn't done his homework.   Yes—No

4. Your classmate is copying from your test paper.   Yes—No

5. Your brother or sister is eating ice cream just before dinner.   Yes—No

6. You find out that your best friend has been shoplifting.   Yes—No

7. Your friend is ill but asks you not to tell his or her parents.   Yes—No

8. Your brother or sister has sneaked out of bed to watch a late movie.   Yes—No

9. One friend tells another that she got straight A's on her report card.   Yes—No
    You know it's not true.

10. Someone you know has been calling in false alarms to the   Yes—No
    fire department.

A Practical Joke

Think of a practical joke that would not harm anyone. Be sure it's a joke that you wouldn't mind if someone played it on you.

Describe your practical joke.

_____

_____

_____

_____

_____

Now draw a picture of the result of the joke.

The Easy Way Out

Eric and Trevor walked home from school together. They talked about the new superhero movie. It was playing in the theater downtown.

"I saw it last night," Trevor said excitedly. "It was really terrific!"

Eric really wanted to see it. Most of his classmates had seen it. They talked about it during recess.

"I heard it was really great," Eric said. "My dad promised to take Donna and me when he has the time."

Trevor told Eric that the movie would be in town for only a few more days. He said that he hoped Eric would get a chance to see it. Eric hoped so too! His father had been working late every night. So far, he hadn't been able to take him and his sister Donna.

When they reached Trevor's house, Trevor said, "I'll meet you in your yard in about twenty minutes."

"Great!" agreed Eric. "Bring your ball and glove. We can have a catch."

As planned, the two boys met in Eric's yard. They played ball for about two hours. Then they both went home for supper.

When Eric got home, his sister Donna and his parents were already seated around the table. Eric joined them. As they ate, Eric and Donna told their parents about what they did at school.

"Have you any homework?" asked their mother.

"I did mine in school," stated Donna.

"So did I," Eric added.

"In that case, I have a surprise for you," replied their father." I came home early tonight so I could take you to see the superhero movie you've been wanting to see!"

Their parents really didn't like them to go out on a school night; however, tonight was their only chance to see it. Their mother explained that it would be past their bedtime when they got home. If Donna and Eric promised to go to bed as soon as they returned, they could go. Of course, they both promised they would!

Eric and Donna were very excited. They ran to their rooms to get ready. Just as Eric was about to put on his jacket, he remembered something. His book report was due tomorrow. He had forgotten all about it!

He'd never be able to write the report and go to the movies too. The report would take at least an hour to write. He knew his parents wouldn't let him work on it after the movie. It would be too late.

Eric didn't know what to do. He thought about not handing in the report, but he was afraid his teacher would be angry. She had warned them that those who didn't hand it in on time better have a good reason; otherwise, they would get a lower grade!

He thought about doing it in the morning. He could get up extra early. Then he remembered how hard it was for him to wake up in the morning— even with the alarm. His mother always had to come in and shake him!

Then a brainstorm hit him! His sister had saved her book reports from last year. He ran to her desk.

Just as he thought. Donna had a report on the very same book he had read. There was even a picture to illustrate it! She had had a different teacher. Eric was sure his teacher wouldn't recognize the report. He had just enough time to copy it over! The book report would be done on time, and he could still go to the movies.

Still, Eric wasn't sure. He knew that to copy someone else's work was cheating. But was this really cheating? After all, he had read the book. He knew what it was about.

Eric thought again about the movie. He really wanted to see it. Whenever his classmates talked about it, he felt left out. Everyone in his class had seen him reading the book. They would all think that he did the report himself. No one would know that he had copied his sister's.

And yet, Eric didn't feel right about it. He didn't know what to do.

What would you do if you were Eric?

Write three possible endings to this story.

Ending #1

_____

_____

_____

_____

_____

Ending #2

_____

_____

_____

_____

_____

Ending #3

_____

_____

_____

_____

_____

Put a ✔ next to the ending that describes what you would do if you were Eric.

Suppose Eric copies his sister's paper and gets caught. What would you say to him as each of the following people:

His teacher: _____

_____

His parents: _____

_____

His sister: _____

_____

If you were Eric's teacher, would you think that going to the movies was a good reason not to hand in the report on time? Why or why not?

_____

_____

_____

Do you think that Eric would be cheating if he copied his sister's paper? Does it make a difference that he read the book?

_____

_____

_____

How would you feel if you really wanted to go someplace but had to stay home to do a report or project that you had known about for a while? Whom would you blame?

_____

_____

_____

Were you ever in a situation where most of your friends had seen a certain movie and you hadn't? How did you feel? Which do you think you cared about more: seeing the movie or being able to join in the conversations about the movie?

_____

_____

_____

*Cheat (chēt), 1 deceive or trick; play or do business in a way that is not honest; *He always cheats at games if he can get away with it.* **2** person who is not honest and does things to deceive and trick others. **3** fraud; trick.
*From the Thorndike Barnhart Beginning Dictionary, 6th edition.

Keeping the above definition in mind, compile a list of the ways in which people cheat.

_____   _____

_____   _____

_____   _____

_____   _____

_____   _____

Draw a series of pictures that show how people cheat: at home, at school, at work and at play.

At Home   **At School**

_____   _____

_____   _____

_____   _____

_____   _____

_____   _____

At Work   **At Play**

_____   _____

_____   _____

_____   _____

_____   _____

_____   _____

C-H-E-A-T-I-N-G

There are more than fifty words that can be formed by using the letters in the word "cheating." How many can you form? Use only words with three or more letters.

1. _____
2. _____
3. _____
4. _____
5. _____
6. _____
7. _____
8. _____
9. _____
10. _____
11. _____
12. _____
13. _____
14. _____
15. _____
16. _____
17. _____

18. _____
19. _____
20. _____
21. _____
22. _____
23. _____
24. _____
25. _____
26. _____
27. _____
28. _____
29. _____
30. _____
31. _____
32. _____
33. _____
34. _____

35. _____
36. _____
37. _____
38. _____
39. _____
40. _____
41. _____
42. _____
43. _____
44. _____
45. _____
46. _____
47. _____
48. _____
49. _____
50. _____

What About Me?

It was Saturday afternoon, and Jeff was feeling good. He planned to spend the afternoon at the park with his friend Trevor—just as he did every Saturday. As soon as Jeff finished his lunch, he grabbed his ball and glove and left for the park. When he arrived, he was surprised to find that Trevor was already playing with someone!

"Hi, Jeff," Trevor said when he saw him. "This is my friend John. He just moved into town." Trevor then explained that he and John had gone to camp together. They had even been in the same bunk.

At first things seemed to go well. The three boys played baseball for a while. They were having a lot of fun! It wasn't until they decided to take a break that things started to change.

Before long John and Trevor were talking about the good times they had at camp. First they talked about their counselors. Then they discussed the other campers in their bunk. The next thing Jeff knew, Trevor had taken out his wallet. In it was a picture of the boys in their bunk. They related stories about each of them one by one!

Jeff didn't want to hear about these people. He didn't know any of them! He wished they would talk about something else.

They did! But the next subject was no better! When Trevor and John finished talking about their camp friends, they began to talk about the camp food.

"I didn't like the pizza too much," Trevor commented.

"I didn't either," agreed John, "but I loved the cookouts! They were great!"

"Yeah," said Trevor, "roasting the marshmallows at the end were the most fun!"

To Jeff's surprise, John turned to him to ask him a question. Finally they were going to include him in the conversation! "Which camp are you going to this summer?" John asked.

"I'm not going to camp," Jeff replied.

John merely said, "Oh," and continued talking to Trevor.

Jeff just listened. Whenever he tried to change the subject, they just started in again about camp. Once they actually stopped long enough for Jeff to ask if they wanted to play ball again. But Trevor and John both said they really didn't feel like it.

Before long they were talking about camp again. This time it was about the bus. First Jeff had to listen to all the silly things they did at the bus stop; however, the worst was yet to come! They sang every song they could think of that they had sung to and from camp. Jeff couldn't join in even if he wanted; he didn't know the words.

By now Jeff really felt left out. He didn't want to hang around while they talked about camp. Jeff wondered why Trevor even bothered to ask him to join them.

Jeff didn't know what to do. Trevor was his best friend. At least he thought he was until now. If he left, Trevor might just start playing with John and forget about him altogether. He wished that John had never moved to the neighborhood. If it weren't for him, Trevor would still be his best friend.

He thought of going to Trevor's house and telling his parents how they were treating him. Then he realized that the boys would probably just call him a crybaby or a tattletale. If might make things worse than they are now!

Maybe he should tell Trevor they way he feels—but what if Trevor didn't care? What if he and John made fun of him?

Jeff didn't know what to do.

What would you do if you were Jeff?

Write three possible endings to this story.

Ending #1

_____

_____

_____

_____

_____

Ending #2

_____

_____

_____

_____

_____

Ending #3

_____

_____

_____

_____

_____

Put a ✔ next to the ending that describes what you would do if you were Jeff.

Do you think Trevor meant to make Jeff feel left out? Why or why not?

_____

_____

_____

Do you think that Jeff would have been a tattletale if he told Trevor's parents? Why or why not?

_____

_____

_____

Do you think Trevor should have been more aware of Jeff's feelings? Why or why not?

_____

_____

_____

Do you think Jeff should have been more understanding about Trevor's wanting to reminisce (to recollect and talk about past experiences) about camp? Why or why not?

_____

_____

_____

Why do you think Trevor and John kept talking about their camp experiences? Do you think the problem will continue for a long time? Why or why not?

_____

_____

_____

Think about a time when you felt left out.
Draw a picture of the situation.

Did you think the others were intentionally making you feel left out?

_____

_____

_____

Do you think so now? If you've changed your mind, tell why.

_____

_____

_____

How did you react?

_____

_____

_____

Would you react the same way again if given the chance?

_____

_____

_____

Think about a situation in which someone you were with felt left out.
Draw a picture of the situation.

Did you or any of the others in your group intentionally make the person feel left out?

_____

_____

_____

Did the person who was hurt feel it was intentional?

_____

_____

_____

How did the person react?

_____

_____

_____

How did you feel when you realized the person felt left out?

_____

_____

_____

What did you do when your realized?

_____

_____

_____

He's Bigger

Neil tossed his baseball in the air as he began his walk home from school. Baseball was his favorite sport. He couldn't wait for the games to start.

Just then he saw Frankie, who was a few years older than he. Neil had heard stories about Frankie from the other children in his class. They said he was always picking on them. Many of his friends were afraid of him. Neil walked the other way, hoping that Frankie wouldn't notice him, but Frankie spotted him right away.

Neil tried not to show his fear when Frankie stopped him in his path.

"Where'd you get that baseball?" Frankie asked.

"I —"

Before Neil had a chance to answer him, Frankie grabbed it away from him. "I need a new baseball," Frankie told him. "I'm going to keep it."

Even though Neil was afraid, he told Frankie that it was his ball and that he wanted it back. Frankie refused to give it to him and dared him to try to take it. Not only that, he also told Neil that the next day he wanted his glove. He threatened to beat him up if he didn't bring it!

"I'm going to tell my parents as soon as I get home," Neil managed to say.

"You'll be sorry," Frankie warned. "You'd better watch out for my friends and me if you do!"

Neil was too frightened to say anything else. He just stood there and watched as Frankie walked away with his baseball. He walked the rest of the way home with his head down, sad and afraid.

That evening Neil hardly touched his dinner. When his mother asked what was wrong, Neil answered that he just wasn't hungry. He had thought about telling his mother and father, but he was afraid of what Frankie and his friends would do. He was also afraid that everyone would think he was a baby for telling his parents. Instead, he just asked to be excused from the table.

That night Neil had trouble sleeping. The little sleep he had was spoiled by bad dreams. When he woke up in the morning, he felt awful. At first he thought he might be getting sick. He soon realized that he wasn't sick. The terrible feeling in his stomach was because he was afraid.

He almost wished he were sick. Then he wouldn't have to go to school and see Frankie. Maybe Frankie would forget about him by the time he went back. For a minute, Neil thought about pretending to be sick and staying home.

Then Neil remembered that his class was going on a field trip. He didn't want to miss it. Besides, he didn't really believe that Frankie would forget about him so easily.

Neil felt awful. He didn't want to give up his baseball glove. It had taken him months to save up enough money to buy it. He wanted his baseball back too. After all, you can't really play baseball with a tennis ball.

He thought of trying to fight Frankie. But Frankie and his friends were much bigger and older than Neil. He didn't think he had much of a chance to win.

Neil also thought of running away at first sight of him. He was one of the best runners in his class. Neil put on his best running shoes, but he knew this wasn't really the answer. After all, he couldn't run forever. Sooner or later Frankie would catch up with him.

Neil looked in the mirror. "Maybe I can disguise myself so that Frankie doesn't know who I am," he said out loud. Of course, he knew that would never work.

Just then he heard his mother calling him for breakfast. The funny feeling in his stomach was still there. He thought of telling his mom and dad what happened. Then he thought of calling Frankie's parents.

But what if they didn't believe him? Worse yet, what if Frankie answered the phone!

Neil didn't know what to do.

What would you do if you were Neil?

Write three possible endings to this story.

Ending #1

_____

_____

_____

_____

_____

Ending #2

_____

_____

_____

_____

_____

Ending #3

_____

_____

_____

_____

_____

Put a ✔ next to the ending that describes what you would do if you were Neil.

Do you think Neil would be a tattletale if he told on Frankie?

_____

_____

_____

What do you think will happen if Neil gives Frankie his glove? Do you think this would solve Neil's problem with Frankie?

_____

_____

_____

Pretend you are Neil's mother or father. What would you say to Neil if he told you what had happened?

_____

_____

_____

Pretend you are Frankie's mother or father. Neil's parents have just told you what happened. What would you say to Frankie?

_____

_____

_____

Do you think all parents would react the same way? Explain.

_____

_____

_____

Look up and write the definition of the word "bully." Does Frankie fit the description? Why do bullies behave the way they do?

_____

_____

_____

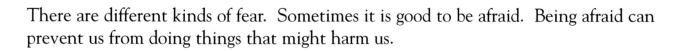

"Fear"

There are different kinds of fear. Sometimes it is good to be afraid. Being afraid can prevent us from doing things that might harm us.

Draw a picture of something that you are afraid of that you have good reason to fear.

Draw a picture of something that you are afraid of that you think you are silly to fear.

Phobias

A phobia is an extreme, illogical fear of a certain object, event, or situation.

See if you can match these phobias with the objects of the fear. Use the hints below if necessary.

PHOBIA	OBJECT OF FEAR
_____ 1. Zoophobia	A. Lizards or Reptiles
_____ 2. Claustrophobia	B. Heights
_____ 3. Aquaphobia	C. Strangers
_____ 4. Xenophobia	D. Animals
_____ 5. Herpetophobia	E. Closed places
_____ 6. Brontophobia	F. Darkness or night
_____ 7. Acrophobia	G. Thunder
_____ 8. Nycotophobia	H. Water
_____ 9. Pyrophobia	I. Cats
_____ 10. Ailurophobia	J. Fire

Hints:
akra = *Greek*, height or summit
ailuros = *Greek*, cat
aqua = *Latin*, water
bronte = *Greek*, thunder
claustrum = *Latin*, bar, bolt or lock
kynas = *Greek*, dog
herpetos = *Greek*, a creeping crawling think
nyx = *Greek*, night
pyr = *Greek*, fire
xenos = *Greek*, stranger
zoos = *Greek*, animals

That Makes Me Mad!

As Taylor was walking home rom school one afternoon, she saw that Jill was waiting for her. She and Jill had been friends since kindergarten. They usually walked home from school together. Today, however, Taylor was not happy to see Jill. In fact, she was furious at her!

That morning on the way to school Jill had begged Taylor to tell her which boy in the class she liked. At first Taylor didn't want to tell her. When Jill promised to keep it a secret, Taylor told her that Jimmy was the one she liked.

Taylor forgot all about her secret until later that day. Patricia, a girl in her class, ran up to her during recess. She teased Taylor about Jimmy being her boyfriend. She said that everyone in the class knew.

Jill was the only one whom Taylor had told. Although Taylor was very angry at Jill for breaking her promise, however, she tried to act as if nothing were wrong. Instead of telling her that she was angry, she hardly said a word.

It didn't take Jill long to realize that something was bothering Taylor. "Do you feel okay?" she asked.

Taylor just answered, "Yes." In fact, whenever Jill asked her a question she merely replied, "Yes," "No," or "I don't know." Inside she was boiling, but she didn't know how to tell Jill how she felt.

Taylor really wanted to get back at Jill for what she had done. She thought about getting Jill to tell her something she wanted to keep secret. Then she would tell the whole world!

When they reached Jill's house, Jill invited her to play with her new frisbee. Taylor accepted, although not very enthusiastically. Jill went in to get it.

Taylor usually enjoyed playing frisbee. She tried not to think about how angry she was, but it was impossible. The longer they played, the angrier she became. She had trusted Jill not to tell and now the whole class knew—even Jimmy! Taylor thought about how hard it would be to talk to him now.

The angrier she became, the harder she threw the frisbee. She purposely threw it so that Jill would have to run around the yard. Then she threw it so that it almost hit Jill. Jill ducked just in time.

"Throw the frisbee *to* me, not *at* me!" Jill yelled.

Finally, Taylor threw the frisbee so wildly that it got stuck on the shed. Jill asked her to get it down.

"If you want it, you'll have to get it yourself," Taylor replied.

Jill was beginning to get angry herself. "Why are you acting this way?" she asked, trying to be patient.

Taylor was tempted to tell her that she wasn't her friend anymore. Then she thought about all the years they had known each other. Besides, she felt a little ashamed of the way she had been behaving. She knew she was being kind of mean.

Taylor didn't think she could go on pretending that everything was okay. She considered telling Jill why she was angry. But what if she teased her? What if she didn't understand why she wanted it to be a secret? She was confused.

Taylor didn't know what to do.

What would you do if you were Taylor?

Write three possible endings to this story.

Ending #1

_____

_____

_____

_____

_____

Ending #2

_____

_____

_____

_____

_____

Ending #3

_____

_____

_____

_____

_____

Put a ✔ next to the ending that describes what you would do if you were Taylor.

Do you think Taylor has a right to be angry at Jill?

_____

_____

_____

Do you think Jill has a right to be angry at Taylor?

_____

_____

_____

Has anyone ever broken a promise to keep one of your secrets? How did you feel? Describe the situation. Did you tell your friend how you felt? How did he or she react?

_____

_____

_____

Have you ever pretended that nothing was wrong when you were annoyed at someone? Was it easy to do?

_____

_____

_____

How do you think Jill would feel if Taylor told her the truth?

_____

_____

_____

When someone tells you a secret, do you keep it? Is it ever okay to break a promise to keep a secret? Under what circumstances would you tell someone's secret?

_____

_____

_____

Anger

We all have feelings of anger from time to time. How we deal with those feelings depends in part at whom the anger is directed. Make up situations in which a person is angry at a parent, a brother or a sister, a friend, and a teacher. Describe how the person might express his/her anger in each.

1. Person is angry at mother or father.

Situation: _____

_____

How anger is expressed: _____

_____

2. Person is angry at brother or sister.

Situation: _____

_____

How anger is expressed: _____

_____

3. Person is angry at friend.

Situation: _____

_____

How anger is expressed: _____

_____

4. Person is angry at teacher.

Situation: _____

_____

How anger is expressed: _____

_____

Pet Peeves

Create a list of your "Pet Peeves."

_____

_____

_____

_____

_____

_____

_____

_____

Draw a picture that illustrates what annoys you the most.

Well, <u>They</u> Did It!

When Kim got out of school, she was very happy. She saw that her new friends Joey, Drew, Stacy, and Denise were waiting for her. They asked if she'd like to walk home with them.

Kim was just starting to get friendly with them. They seemed to enjoy the same kinds of things as she. Today during lunch break they all played ball together. She especially liked Joey's sense of humor. He was always doing funny things that made her laugh.

As they walked down the street, they linked arms and called themselves the "Fearless Five." "Let's play 'Don't Step on the Crack,' " suggested Stacy. They all hopped from one square to another.

Kim was having such a good time that she didn't realize which way they were walking. Suddenly she noticed that they were headed in the direction of the railroad tracks. Her parents had told her never to walk on the tracks. They had said it was very dangerous. She had promised them that she wouldn't go near the tracks. Kim hoped that they would turn the corner before reaching them.

Just as they were about to turn, Joey said that he had a great idea. "Let's walk on the tracks and see if we can balance ourselves," he said enthusiastically.

"That sounds like fun," Stacy replied. Denise and Drew agreed.

Kim remembered her parents' warning. "Isn't that kind of dangerous?" she asked shyly.

"Nothing is too dangerous for the Fearless Five," Joey responded.

"Besides," Drew said to reassure her, "We've done it before and nothing's happened."

Kim was worried. She didn't want to break the promise she had made to her mother and father. On the other hand, she didn't want to tell her new friends that she couldn't join them. What if they thought she was a baby? What if they didn't want to play with her anymore?

She tried to make another suggestion. "Do you want to turn down this street?" she asked. "We could stop for a soda at the candy store down the block."

"I don't care," said Drew. "I am kind of thirsty. I could go for a soda."

But Stacy and Denise both said that it wasn't as much fun as walking on the tracks. Joey agreed. They kept on walking towards the tracks. Kim trailed behind.

Joey ran ahead to see if it was clear. When he decided that it was, he called for the others to come.

Kim didn't want to disobey her parents. She thought about telling her friends that she wasn't allowed to go with them. She could go the other way and meet them when they got off the tracks.

She wasn't sure what to do. Kim was embarrassed to tell them the truth. They might make fun of her and not want to be her friend. Besides, she wondered why they were allowed to go and she wasn't.

They called to her to hurry!

Kim didn't know what to do.

What would you do if you were Kim?

Write three possible endings to this story.

Ending #1

_____

_____

_____

_____

_____

Ending #2

_____

_____

_____

_____

_____

Ending #3

_____

_____

_____

_____

_____

Put a ✔ next to the ending that describes what you would do if you were Kim.

Do you think Kim would have felt differently if she had been friendly with these children for a long time? Why or why not?

_____

_____

_____

Were your friends ever allowed to do something that you weren't allowed to do? How did you feel? Did you think that you should have been allowed to do it?

_____

_____

_____

Have you ever done anything because your friends were doing it even though you thought it was a bad idea? How did you feel?

_____

_____

_____

Pretend that you are grown up and have children of your own. Complete the following conversation from the point of view of you as a parent.

12-year-old Child: We're all taking the day off from school tomorrow and taking the bus into the city to see the parade.

You as Parent: First of all, you're too young to go into the city without an adult. Secondly, you may not miss a day of school to go to a parade.

Child: But everyone else's parents are letting them go!

You:

_____

_____

_____

_____

How Would You React?

For each situation, fill in the way you would react.

A.

Have one of my cigarettes, Bill. Come on, everyone smokes.

Bill: _____

_____

_____

_____

_____

_____

B.

We're all cutting class to go to the movies. We'll meet you downtown. Okay, Sue?

Sue: _____

_____

_____

_____

_____

_____

C.

Come on, Mike, get in. I'll have my license in a few weeks anyway!"

Mike: _____

_____

_____

_____

_____

_____

Have a Mind of Your Own!

It takes courage and confidence to decide not to follow when you believe the others are wrong. On this page write a story about someone who has the courage not to go along with the crowd.

_____

_____

_____

_____

_____

_____

_____

_____

_____

_____

_____

_____

_____

_____

_____

_____

_____

_____

Answers

"I Wish I Hadn't Said That"

Scrambled Words

1. lie
2. fib
3. half-truth
4. falsehood
5. deception
6. untruth
7. white lie
8. prevaricate
9. equivocate
10. perjury

"He's Bigger"

Phobias

1. D
2. E
3. H
4. C
5. A
6. G
7. B
8. F
9. J
10. I

"The Easy Way Out"

C-H-E-A-T-I-N-G

1. ace
2. age
3. ant
4. ate
5. cage
6. can
7. cane
8. cat
9. chain
10. chat
11. cheat
12. chin
13. each
14. eat
15. eating
16. eight
17. gain
18. gait
19. gate
20. get
21. giant
22. gin
23. gnat
24. hag
25. hang
26. hat
27. hate
28. hating
29. heat
30. heating
31. hen
32. hinge
33. hint
34. hit
35. inch
36. itch
37. net
38. nice
39. niche
40. nigh
41. night
42. tag
43. tan
44. tang
45. tea
46. teach
47. ten
48. than
49. the
50. then
51. thin
52. thing
53. tie
54. tin
55. tinge

Emotion Word Search

Create your own word search using words that describe feelings. Remember, words can go across, backwards, up, down, or diagonally. Write the words used in the space at the bottom of the page. Be sure to fill in the extra spaces with letters.

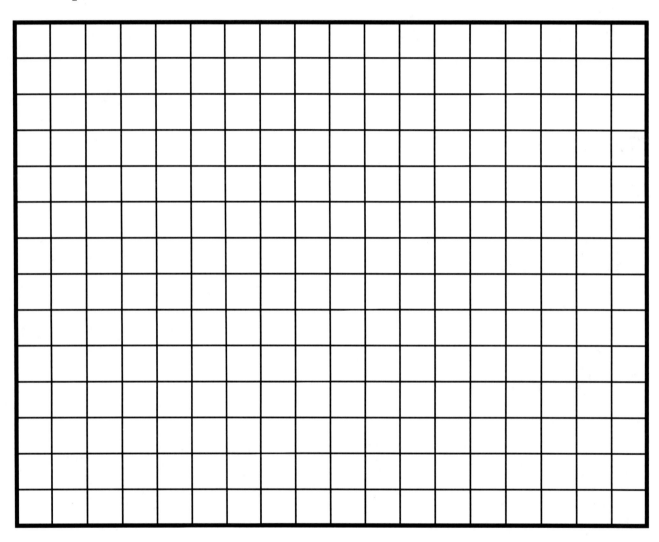

Word List

_____   _____   _____

_____   _____   _____

_____   _____   _____

_____   _____   _____

Story Starters

Look at each picture. Make up a story about each. Tell what happened before the picture was taken. What is happening now? What will happen to the characters in the pictures?

_____

_____

_____

_____

_____

_____

_____

_____

_____

_____

_____

_____

_____

_____

_____

_____

_____

_____

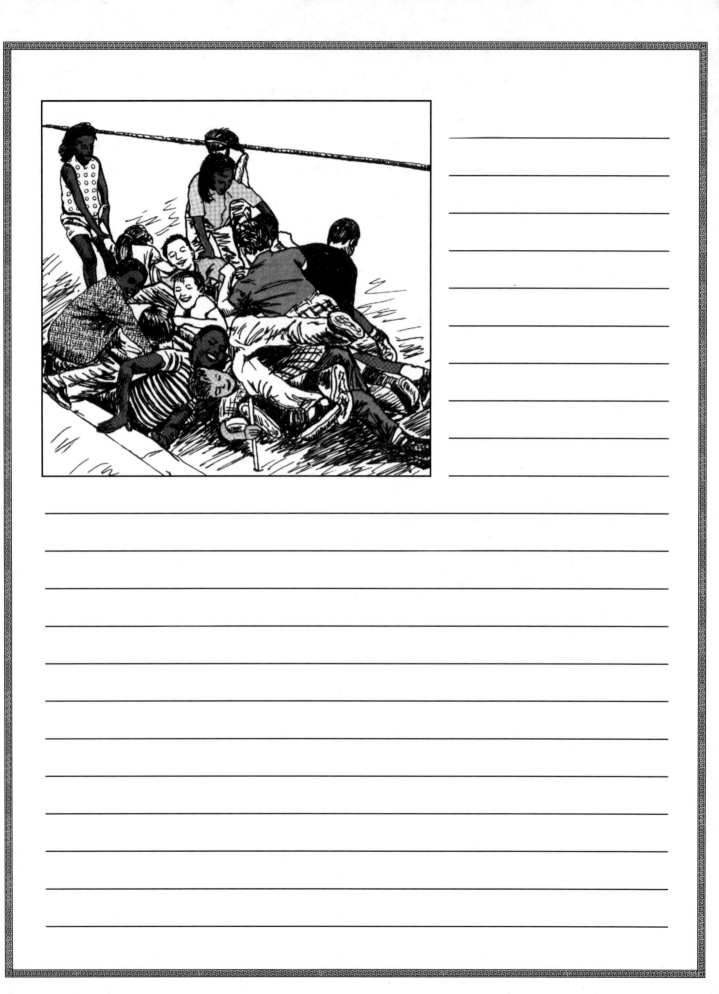